MY VEGAN SMOOTHIES AND JUICES

Sabat Beatto

COPYRIGHT

The information presented in this report solely and fully represents the views of the author as of the date of publication. Any omission, or potential Misrepresentation of, any peoples or companies, is entirely unintentional. As a result of changing information, conditions or contexts, this author reserves the right to alter content at their sole discretion impunity. The report is for informational purposes only and while every attempt has been made to verify the informationcontained herein, the author, assumes no responsibility for errors, inaccuracies, and omissions.Each person has unique needs and this book cannot take these individual differences in account.

This e-book is copyright © 2019 by the Author with all rights reserved. It is illegal to copy, distribute, or create derivative works from this ebook inwhole or in part. No part of this report may be reproduced or transmitted in any form whatsoever, electronic, or mechanical, including photocopying, recording, or by any informational storage or retrieval system without expressed written, dated and signed permission from the author.

MY VEGAN SMOOTHIES AND JUICES

TABLE OF CONTENTS

1. RED ROOSTER SMOOTHIE 5
2. WATERMELON SMOOTHIE COOLER 7
3. BOMBAY BANANA SMOOTHIE 8
4. CAN'T BEET THIS SMOOTHIE 10
5. POPEYE BANANA SMOOTHIE 12
6. CHERRY ALMOND SMOOTHIE 14
7. BERRY IMMUNITY SMOOTHIE 16
8. RASPBERRY GREEN SMOOTHIE 18
9. PUMPKIN CHAI SMOOTHIE 19
10. PEARRIFIC SMOOTHIE 21
11. PUMPKIN ORANGE CREAM SMOOTHIE 23
12. BANANA BREAD SUPER FOODS SMOOTHIE 25
13. APPLE PIE GREEN SMOOTHIE 27
14. SLEEPY STRAWBERRY CHEESECAKE SMOOTHIE 29
15. GREEN ENERGY SMOOTHIE 31
16. MINT CHOCOLATE CHIP SMOOTHIE 32
17. BLUSHING APPLE SMOOTHIE 34
18. SLEEPY BLUEBERRY MUFFIN SMOOTHIE 35
19. SLEEPY RASPBERRY LEMON POPPY SEED SMOOTHIE 37
20. ENERGY SMOOTHIES 39
21. SLEEPY BANANA MUFFIN SMOOTHIE 41
22. PUMPKIN SPICE SMOOTHIE 43
23. SLEEPY CHOCOLATE CHIP COOKIE DOUGH SMOOTHIE 45
24. CARAMEL APPLE GREEN SMOOTHIE 47

MY VEGAN SMOOTHIES AND JUICES

25. KEY LIME PIE GREEN SMOOTHIE 49

26. SUPERWOMAN GREEN SMOOTHIE 51

27. VEGAN SNICKERS SHAKE 53

28. CANTALOUPE LEMON AGUA FRESCA 54

29. SO-HEALTHY SMOOTHIES 56

30. AVOCADO STRAWBERRY LAYERED SMOOTHIE 57

31. STRAWBERRY-CARROT SMOOTHIES 59

32. PEACH GREEN TEA SMOOTHIE 60

33. HEALTHY CHOCOLATE BANANA SMOOTHIE 61

34. RASPBERRY ALMOND SMOOTHIE 63

35. CARROT GINGER TURMERIC SMOOTHIE 65

36. CUCUMBER-MELON SMOOTHIE 67

37. THE CREAMIEST BANANA CINNAMON ROLL SMOOTHIE 68

38. VEGAN STRAWBERRY PUDDING 70

39. HOMEMADE OAT MILK 71

40. HEALING CRANBERRY SMOOTHIE 72

1. RED ROOSTER SMOOTHIE

Ingredients
- 1 cup water
- 6 strawberries
- 2 slices of raw red beet, chopped (approx. 2 tablespoons)
- 15 green grapes
- ½ cucumber, skin removed
- ½ orange, skin removed
- 2 large handfuls of spinach
- 4-6 ice cubes

Total time
40 seconds

Direction
Add all ingredients to the jug of your blender in the order they are listed and blend for 20-30 seconds, until smooth.
Serve immediately.

Nutrition Information
Calories:150
Calories from Fat:4.5
Total Fat:0.5 g
Sodium:23 mg
Carbs:36.9 g
Dietary Fiber:2 g
Net Carbs:34.9 g
Sugars:27.1 g
Protein:2.3 g

2. WATERMELON SMOOTHIE COOLER

Ingredient
- 2 cups cubed watermelon
- 5 frozen strawberries
- ½ cup coconut water

Prep Time:
5 minutes
Serves:1

Directions
Add all ingredients to your blender and blend until smooth.

Nutrition Information
Calories:150
Calories from Fat:4.5
Total Fat:0.5 g
Sodium:23 mg
Carbs:36.9 g
Dietary Fiber:2 g
Net Carbs:34.9 g
Sugars:27.1 g
Protein:2.3 g

3. BOMBAY BANANA SMOOTHIE

Ingredients

- 1 cup non-dairy milk – I used unsweetened almond milk
- 1 medium banana
- 1 teaspoon creamed coconut or coconut butter
- 2 medjool dates, pitted
- ½ teaspoon chai spice (also known as chai or tea masala)
- 1 knob of fresh ginger, skin removed (yield ~ 1 teaspoon)

Prep Time:
5 minutes
Serves: 1

Directions
Place in your blender in the order of the ingredients listed.
Blend for 30 seconds or until smooth.

Nutrition Information
Calories: 298
Calories from Fat: 59.4

Total Fat:6.6 g
Saturated Fat:3 g
Sodium:182 mg
Carbs:61.4 g
Dietary Fiber:8.1 g
Net Carbs:53.3 g
Sugars:40.5 g
Protein:4.2 g

4. CAN'T BEET THIS SMOOTHIE

Ingredients

- 2 apples, juiced (2/3 cup apple juice)
- 1 large beet juiced (about 3 tablespoons)
- 1 cup mixed frozen berries
- 1/2 banana

Prep Time:
5 minutes
Serves: 1

Instructions

Place all ingredients in your blender in the order listed, then blend for 30 seconds or until smooth.

Nutrition Information
Calories:237
Calories from Fat:9.9
Total Fat:1.1 g
Sodium:29 mg
Carbs:58.5 g
Dietary Fiber:6.7 g
Net Carbs:51.8 g
Sugars:43.3 g
Protein:2.4 g

5. POPEYE BANANA SMOOTHIE

Ingredients

- 1/2 cup water
- 1/2 cup vanilla goat dairy yogurt or non-dairy yogurt
- 1/2 banana
- 2 handfuls fresh spinach
- 1 tablespoon raw almonds
- 1/4 teaspoon almond extract

Prep Time:
5 minutes
Serves: 1

Directions
Place in your blender in the order of the ingredients listed, then blend for 30 seconds or until smooth. Enjoy!

Nutrition Information
Calories:191
Calories from Fat:44.1
Total Fat:4.9 g
Saturated Fat:1.6 g
Cholesterol:7 mg
Sodium:137 mg
Carbs:25.7 g
Dietary Fiber:3.6 g
Net Carbs:22.1
Sugars:16.4 g
Protein:10.6 g

6. CHERRY ALMOND SMOOTHIE

Ingredients

- 1 cup pitted cherries, fresh or frozen
- 1 scoop vanilla protein powder
- 2 teaspoon almond butter
- 1 teaspoon pure almond extract
- 1/2 teaspoon maca root powder (optional – doesn't affect the taste or texture)
- 1/2 teaspoon camu camu powder a powerful super food with lots of anti-inflammatory and anti-oxidant properties (optional)
- 1 cup water or unsweetened almond milk
- 6-8 ice cubes ice
- 1/2 teaspoon guar gum to enhance creaminess (optional)

Prep Time:
10 minutes
Serves: 1

Directions

Place all ingredients in a blender except for the ice and guar gum. Blend until almost smooth.

Add ice and guar gum, and continue blending. Pour into glasses and enjoy!

Nutrition Information
Calories:257
Calories from Fat:79.2
Total Fat:8.8 g
Saturated Fat:1.2 g
Cholesterol:37 mg
Sodium:38 mg
Carbs:21.8 g
Dietary Fiber:3 g
Net Carbs:18.8 g
Sugars:15.1 g
Protein:25.4 g

7. BERRY IMMUNITY SMOOTHIE

Ingredients

- 2 tablespoons unsweetened cranberry sauce
- 1 tablespoon of chia seed, flax seed or hemp seed
- 1/2 cup homemade apple juice
- 1/2 fresh or frozen banana
- 1/2 cup fresh or frozen blueberries
- 1/2 cup tightly packed kale leaves

Prep Time:
5 minutes
Serves: 1

Instructions

Place all ingredients in your blender in the order listed, then blend for 30 seconds or until smooth.

Nutrition Information

Calories:227
Calories from Fat:52.2
Total Fat:5.8 g
Saturated Fat:0.5 g
Sodium:19 mg
Carbs:48 g
Dietary Fiber:9.6 g
Net Carbs:38.4 g
Sugars:27.3 g
Protein:5.4 g

MY VEGAN SMOOTHIES AND JUICES

8. RASPBERRY GREEN SMOOTHIE

Ingredients

- 1 cup non-dairy milk
- 1 ripe pear, sliced with core removed
- 1 cup frozen raspberries
- 1 cup baby spinach
- 2 leaves kale
- 1/2 teaspoon gluten-free pure vanilla extract

Prep Time:
5 minutes
Serves: 1

Directions
Place all ingredients in your blender in the order listed and blend for 30 seconds or until smooth.

Nutrition Information
Calories:215
Calories from Fat:36.9
Total Fat:4.1 g
Sodium:235 mg
Carbs:45 g
Dietary Fiber:15.3 g
Net Carbs:29.7 g
Sugars:19.2 g
Protein:6.1 g

9. PUMPKIN CHAI SMOOTHIE

Ingredients
- 1½ cup non-dairy milk – I used unsweetened almond milk
- ½ cup canned or fresh pureed pumpkin
- 1 medium banana, frozen
- 1 tablespoon chia seeds
- 2 medjool dates, pitted
- 1 knob of fresh ginger
- 1 ½ teaspoon homemade chai spice
- ½ teaspoon pure gluten-free vanilla extract
- 4 ice cubes

Prep Time:
5 minutes
Serves: 1

Directions

Place all ingredients in your blender in the order listed, then blend for 30 seconds or until smooth.

Nutrition Information

Calories:418
Calories from Fat:130.5
Total Fat:14.5 g
Saturated Fat:1.3 g
Sodium:276 mg
Carbs:65.4 g
Dietary Fiber:20.4 g
Net Carbs:45 g
Sugars:31.3 g
Protein:10.8 g

10. PEARRIFIC SMOOTHIE

Ingredients

- 2 kale leaves
- 2 celery sticks
- 2 carrots
- 1 small knob ginger
- 1 pear, core removed and sliced
- 2 cups spinach
- 1 tablespoon chia seeds
- 6-8 ice cubes

Prep Time:
1 minute
Serves: 1

Directions

If you have a 'low' setting on your juicer, begin with the softer items first – kale. Then turn to 'high' and juice the celery, carrots and ginger.

Place fresh juice in the blender with spinach, pear slices, chia seeds and ice.Blend until smooth, about 30 seconds.

Nutrition Information

Calories:258
Calories from Fat:54
Total Fat:6 g
Saturated Fat:0.8 g
Sodium:175 mg
Carbs:47.8 g
Dietary Fiber:11.8 g
Net Carbs:36 g
Sugars:19.9 g
Protein:8.7 g

11. PUMPKIN ORANGE CREAM SMOOTHIE

Ingredients
- 1 medium orange, peeled and sliced
- 1/2 cup vanilla non-dairy yogurt
- 1/2 cup canned pumpkin puree
- 1/2 cup unsweetened orange juice
- 1 tablespoon sweetener – raisins, medjool dates, maple syrup, coconut nectar, etc.
- 1 tablespoon freshly ground flax seed
- 1 small knob ginger
- 1/4 teaspoon ground cinnamon
- Splash alcohol-free vanilla extract
- Pinch ground cloves

Prep Time:
5 minutes
Serves: 1

Directions

Place all ingredients in your blender in the order listed and blend for 30 seconds or until smooth.

Nutrition Information

Calories:347
Calories from Fat:55.8
Total Fat:6.2 g
Saturated Fat:0.5 g
Sodium:29 mg
Carbs:72.3 g
Dietary Fiber:12.2 g
Net Carbs:60.1 g
Sugars:45.2 g
Protein:9.4 g

12. BANANA BREAD SUPER FOODS SMOOTHIE

Ingredients

- 1 cup water
- 1 banana, frozen
- 1/3 cup cooked quinoa or buckwheat
- 1 tablespoon raw walnuts or hemp seeds
- 2 teaspoon cold-pressed flax oil
- 1 medjool date, pitted
- flesh from 1 vanilla bean or ½ teaspoon alcohol-free pure vanilla extract
- ¾ teaspoon ground cinnamon
- pinch allspice
- extra walnuts and ground cinnamon for topping

Prep Time:
5 minutes
Serves: 1

Direction

Place in your blender in the order of the ingredients listed, then blend for 30 seconds or until smooth. Pour into a glass and top with additional walnuts and ground cinnamon.

Nutrition Information

Calories:354
Calories from Fat:144
Total Fat:16 g
Saturated Fat:1.5 g
Sodium:10 mg
Carbs:53 g
Dietary Fiber:6.9 g
Net Carbs:46.1 g
Sugars:23.8 g
Protein:5.9 g

13. APPLE PIE GREEN SMOOTHIE

Ingredients
- 1/2 cup water
- 1/2 cup unsweetened unpasteurized apple juice
- 1 tablespoon walnuts
- 1/2 teaspoon ground cinnamon
- 1/4 teaspoon vanilla extract or maple extract
- pinch ground nutmeg
- 1/2 English cucumber
- 2 cups spinach
- 1 apple, chopped and frozen
- 1/4 avocado, chopped and frozen
- 4-6 ice cubes

Prep Time:
5 minutes
Serves: 1

Direction

Place in your blender in the order of the ingredients listed, then blend for 30 seconds or until smooth.

Nutrition Information

Calories:314
Calories from Fat:115.2
Total Fat:12.8 g
Saturated Fat:1.5 g
Sodium:62 mg
Carbs:50.8 g
Dietary Fiber:10.8 g
Net Carbs:40 g
Sugars:34.6 g
Protein:5.7 g

14. SLEEPY STRAWBERRY CHEESECAKE SMOOTHIE

Ingredients
- 1 cup strawberries
- 1 cup non-dairy milk – I used unsweetened almond milk
- 3 tablespoon uncontaminated oats
- 1 tablespoon chia seed
- 1 tablespoon cashews
- 1 teaspoon apple cider vinegar
- 1 teaspoon lemon juice
- 1/2 teaspoon vanilla
- Pinch stevia

Prep Time:
5 minutes
Serves: 1

Directions
To be made the night before you plan on eating it, or at least 4 hours in advance.

Combine all ingredients in a glass container [I like to use mason jars and give it a quick shake] and place in the fridge overnight.

In the morning, pour ingredients into blender and process until smooth.

Top with cashews + strawberries

Nutrition Information
Calories:224
Calories from Fat:90
Total Fat:10 g
Saturated Fat:1.2 g
Sodium:184 mg
Carbs:28.4 g
Dietary Fiber:7.3 g
Net Carbs:21.1 g
Sugars:8.8 g
Protein:6.9 g

15. GREEN ENERGY SMOOTHIE

Ingredient

- 1 cucumber, seeded and sliced
- 3 cups raw spinach
- 2 cups honeydew melon, cubed [about 1/2 a medium sized melon]
- 1 cup organic green tea
- 1 teaspoon lemon juice
- 1/2 inch fresh ginger root

Prep Time:
5 minutes
Serves: 2

Directions
Blend and enjoy!

Nutrition Information
Calories:67
Calories from Fat:6.3
Total Fat:0.7 g
Sodium:78 mg
Carbs:14.3 g
Dietary Fiber:3.5 g
Net Carbs:10.8 g
Sugars:8 g
Protein:4.6 g

MY VEGAN SMOOTHIES AND JUICES

16 . MINT CHOCOLATE CHIP SMOOTHIE

Ingredients

- 1/2 cup boiling water
- 1 peppermint tea bag
- 1/2 cup non dairy milk – I used unsweetened rice milk
- 2 cups spinach
- 1 medium frozen banana
- 2 tablespoon hemp hearts
- 6 ice cubes
- 3 tablespoon non-dairy chocolate chips, divided

Prep Time:
5 minutes
Serves: 1

Direction
To be prepared at least 30 minutes in advance:
Steep the tea in the 1/2 cup boiling water until ready to use in the

smoothie so that it's really concentrated. Wait until the water has cooled, about 30 minutes. I just make my tea at night and let it sit on the counter overnight.

Place all ingredients but chocolate chips in your blender in the order of the ingredients listed. blend for 30 seconds or until smooth.

Drop in half of the chocolate chips and pulse quickly.

Pour into a cup and top with leftover chocolate.

Nutrition Information
Calories:329
Calories from Fat:95.4
Total Fat:10.6 g
Saturated Fat:2.7 g
Sodium:101 mg
Carbs:52.1 g
Dietary Fiber:7.1 g
Net Carbs:45 g
Sugars:26.9 g
Protein:9.3 g

MY VEGAN SMOOTHIES AND JUICES

17. BLUSHING APPLE SMOOTHIE

Ingredients

- ½ cup pitted fresh cherries
- ½ English cucumber
- 1 apple
- ½ cup fresh raspberries
- 1 tablespoon chia seed
- ½ cup water
- 6-8 ice cubes

Prep Time:
5 minutes
Serves: 2

Direction
Place in your blender in the order of the ingredients listed, then blend for 30 seconds or until smooth.

Nutrition Information
Calories:175
Calories from Fat:273 g
Sodium:15 mg
Carbs:37.9 g
Dietary Fiber:7.4 g
Net Carbs:30.5 g
Sugars:12.1 g
Protein:2.8 g

18. SLEEPY BLUEBERRY MUFFIN SMOOTHIE

Ingredients
- 1 1/2 cup non-dairy milk
- 1/2 cup blueberries
- 2 tablespoon uncontaminated regular oats – alternatively you can use packaged gluten free oatmeal, gluten free granola, or quinoa flakes
- 1 teaspoon pure vanilla extract
- 1 tablespoon vanilla protein powder
- 1 tablespoon chia seed

Prep Time:
5 minutes
Serves: 1

Direction
To be made the night before you plan on eating it, or at least 4 hours in advance.
Night before: combine all ingredients [but the blueberries] in a glass or plastic container. Stir to combine and place in fridge.

Morning: pour contents of container into blender, add blueberries and blend until smooth.

Nutrition Information
Calories:256
Calories from Fat:67.5
Total Fat:7.5 g
Sodium:326 mg
Carbs:13.5 g
Dietary Fiber:7 g
Net Carbs:6.5 g
Sugars:0.9 g
Protein:31.9 g

19. SLEEPY RASPBERRY LEMON POPPY SEED SMOOTHIE

Ingredients

- 1 1/2 cup non-dairy milk –
- 1/2 cup raspberries
- 2 tablespoon uncontaminated rolled oats
- 1 tablespoon lemon juice
- 1 tablespoon almond butter
- 1 tablespoon chia seeds
- 1 1/2 teaspoon poppy seeds
- 1 teaspoon pure vanilla extract
- zest from 1 small lemon
- pinch white stevia powder

Prep Time:
5 minutes
Serves: 1

Direction
To be made the night before you plan on eating it, or at least 4 hours in advance.

Combine all ingredients in a glass container [I like to use mason jars and give it a quick shake] and place in the fridge overnight.

In the morning, pour ingredients into blender and process until smooth.

Nutrition Information
Calories:266
Calories from Fat:162.9
Total Fat:18.1 g
Saturated Fat:1.5 g
Sodium:276 mg
Carbs:20 g
Dietary Fiber:9.6 g
Net Carbs:10.4 g
Sugars:4.2 g
Protein:8.8 g

20. ENERGY SMOOTHIES

Ingredients
Strawberry banana flavor
- 1/2 banana
- 6 strawberries
- 1 cup green tea
- 1 scoop protein powder
- 1 tablespoon chia seeds
- 1 serving probiotics

Blueberry peach flavor
- 1/2 peach
- 1 cup blueberries
- 1 cup green tea
- 1 scoop protein powder
- 1 tablespoon chia seeds
- 1 serving probiotics

Prep Time:
5 minutes
Serves: 1

Direction

Choose a flavor, or prepare both. They stay well in the fridge for 2 days, so you can make both ahead of time.

Combine all ingredients in a 1L mason jar. Seal and place in the fridge overnight.

In the morning, place contents in a blender and blend to your hearts content.

Enjoy!

Nutrition Information

Calories:257
Calories from Fat:60.3
Total Fat:6.7 g
Saturated Fat:1.6 g
Sodium:121 mg
Carbs:27.9 g
Dietary Fiber:7.5 g
Net Carbs:20.4 g
Sugars:14.1 g
Protein:25.1 g

21. SLEEPY BANANA MUFFIN SMOOTHIE

Ingredients

- 1 cup non-dairy milk + 1/4 cup for blending
- 1 frozen banana
- 2 tablespoon uncontaminated regular oats
- 1 tablespoon raisins
- 1/2 teaspoon pure vanilla extract
- 1 tablespoon raw walnuts
- pinch of ground cinnamon
- Optional toppings: coconut, raisins, walnuts, or chocolate chips

Prep Time:
5 minutes
Serves: 1

Direction
Night before: combine all ingredients [but the frozen banana and 1/4 cup milk] in a glass or plastic container. Stir to combine and place in fridge. Morning: pour contents of container into blender, add banana and additional milk, blend until smooth.

Nutrition Information

Calories:256
Calories from Fat:73.8
Total Fat:8.2 g
Saturated Fat:0.5 g
Sodium:183 mg
Carbs:43.3 g
Dietary Fiber:6.1 g
Net Carbs:37.2 g
Sugars:20.3 g
Protein:5.8 g

22. PUMPKIN SPICE SMOOTHIE

Ingredients

- 1 cup non-dairy milk
- 1/2 cup canned pumpkin
- 1/2 banana
- 1 tablespoon raisins or 1/2 teaspoon maple syrup
- 1/2 teaspoon pure vanilla extract
- 1/4 teaspoon ground cinnamon
- 1/8 teaspoon ground ginger
- pinch ground nutmeg
- pinch ground cloves
- pinch all spice
- vegan coconut whipped topping

Prep Time:
5 minutes
Serves: 1

Direction

Place everything but whipped topping in the blender.Blend until smooth Pour into your favorite glass and place a couple tablespoons of coconut whipped cream on top.

Sprinkle with cinnamon if you'd like!

Nutrition Information

Calories:212
Calories from Fat:93.6
Total Fat:10.4 g
Saturated Fat:6.7 g
Sodium:193 mg
Carbs:29.5 g
Dietary Fiber:7.2 g
Net Carbs:22.3g
Sugars:14.6 g
Protein:3.8 g

23. SLEEPY CHOCOLATE CHIP COOKIE DOUGH SMOOTHIE

Ingredients

- 1 cup non-dairy milk + 1/4 cup for blending – I used unsweetened almond milk
- 6 tablespoon uncontaminated oats
- 1 tablespoon chia seeds
- 1 tablespoon almond butter
- 1 tablespoon cacao powder
- 1/4 teaspoon pure vanilla extract

Prep Time:
5 minutes
Serves: 1

Direction
To be made the night before you plan on eating it, or at least 4 hours in advance.
Combine all ingredients in a glass container [I like to use mason jars and give it a quick shake] and place in the fridge overnight.

In the morning, pour ingredients into blender, add additional 1/4 cup milk, and process until smooth.
Top with cacao nibs + coconut

Nutrition Information
Calories:244
Calories from Fat:147.6
Total Fat:16.4 g
Saturated Fat:2 g
Cholesterol:184 mg
Sodium:184 mg
Carbs:20.2 g
Dietary Fiber:7.1 g
Net Carbs:13.1 g
Sugars:0.6 g
Protein:9.1 g

24. CARAMEL APPLE GREEN SMOOTHIE

Ingredients

- 1 cup non-dairy milk
- 1 apple, chopped and frozen
- 2 tablespoon sunbutter
- 2 cups spinach
- 2 medjool dates, pitted
- 1/4 teaspoon pure vanilla extract
- 1/8 teaspoon ground cinnamon
- pinch salt
- 2 ice cubes

Prep Time:

5 minutes

Serves: 1

Direction

Place in your blender in the order of the ingredients listed, then blend for 30 seconds or until smooth.

Nutrition Information
Calories:505
Calories from Fat:169.2
Total Fat:18.8 g
Saturated Fat:1.7 g
Sodium:464 mg
Carbs:81.8 g
Dietary Fiber:11 g
Net Carbs:70.8 g
Sugars:58.4 g
Protein:10.9 g

25. KEY LIME PIE GREEN SMOOTHIE

Ingredients

- 2 tablespoon key lime juice (about 4 limes)
- 1 teaspoon key lime zest (about 2 limes)
- 1 cup unsweetened non-dairy milk
- 1 ripe frozen banana
- ¼ teaspoon alcohol-free vanilla extract
- 2 drops liquid stevia or 1 tablespoon ground xylitol or 1 pitted medjool date
- 1 tablespoon sunflower butter
- 2 cups organic baby spinach
- 4 ice cubes
- 1 minute vanilla whipped topping (optional)
- gluten-free graham cracker pieces (optional)

Prep Time:
5 minutes
Serves: 1

Directions

Place in your blender in the order of the ingredients listed, then blend for 30 seconds or until smooth.

Nutrition Information

Calories:293
Calories from Fat:101.7
Total Fat:11.3 g
Saturated Fat:1 g
Sodium:230 mg
Carbs:51 g
Dietary Fiber:6.4 g
Net Carbs:44.6 g
Sugars:15.4 g
Protein:7.4 g

26. SUPERWOMAN GREEN SMOOTHIE

Ingredients

- 1 cup unsweetened non-dairy milk
- 1 cup spinach
- 1 tablespoon cacao powder
- 1 tablespoon almond butter
- 1 tablespoon coconut oil
- 1 tablespoon unpasteurized honey
- 1 teaspoon spirulina
- 1 cup frozen mixed berries
- 3-6 ice cubes

Prep Time:
5 minutes
Serves: 1

Direction
Place in your blender in the order of the ingredients listed, then blend for 30 seconds or until smooth.

Nutrition Information
Calories:419
Calories from Fat:251.1
Total Fat:27.9 g
Saturated Fat:13.4 g
Sodium:231 mg
Carbs:43.8 g
Dietary Fiber:8.9 g
Net Carbs:34.9 g
Sugars:27.5 g
Protein:7.6 g

27. VEGAN SNICKERS SHAKE

Ingredients

- 1 frozen banana, cut into large chunks
- 3/4–1 cup unsweetened vanilla milk
- 3 pitted dates
- 2 tbsp. peanut butter
- 1/8 tsp. vanilla extract
- 1 1/2 tsp. unsweetened cocoa powder

Total Time:
5 minutes
Prep Time:
5 minutes

Direction
Place the dates and 1/4 cup milk into a high powered blender and puree until the dates have broken down. Add the rest of the ingredients, starting with 1/2 cup almond milk you can always add more if you want it thinner. Add 4-5 ice cubes and puree until ice crushed.
Serve cold.

28. CANTALOUPE LEMON AGUA FRESCA

Ingredients

- 4 cups cantaloupe
- 4 cups water
- 1 large lemon, juiced
- 2–3 tablespoons sugar*
- small pinch salt

Total Time:
5 minutes
Prep Time:
5 minutes
Yield: 6 cups

Directions
Place all ingredients in a large blender and puree until smooth. Strain, using either a nut milk bag or fine mesh strainer.

Nutritional facts

Serves 6
Serving Size: 1 cup
Calories Per Serving: 54
% Daily Value
0% Total Fat 0.2g
Saturated Fat 0.1g
0% Cholesterol 0mg
2% Sodium 47.1mg
4% Total Carbohydrate 13.4g
4% Dietary Fiber 1g
Sugars 12.6g
2% Protein 0.9g
1% Calcium 14.8mg
1% Iron 0.2mg
1% Zinc 0.2mg
6% Folic Acid (B9) 23.9μg

MY VEGAN SMOOTHIES AND JUICES

29. SO-HEALTHY SMOOTHIES

Ingredients

- 1 cup fat-free milk
- 1/4 cup orange juice
- 2 tablespoons vanilla yogurt
- 1 tablespoon honey
- 1 small banana, sliced and frozen
- 2/3 cup frozen blueberries
- 1/2 cup chopped peeled mango, frozen
- 1-1/4 cups frozen unsweetened sliced peaches

Total Time

Prep/Total Time: 15 min.
Makes
4 servings

Directions

In a blender, combine all ingredients; cover and process until smooth. Pour into chilled glasses; serve immediately.

Nutrition Facts

3/4 cup: 107 calories, 1g fat (0 saturated fat), 2mg cholesterol, 38mg sodium, 24g carbohydrate (21g sugars, 2g fiber), 3g protein. Diabetic Exchanges: 1 fruit, 1/2 starch.

30. AVOCADO STRAWBERRY LAYERED SMOOTHIE

Ingredients
Strawberry Smoothie:
- 120 ml (1/2 cup) water
- 225 grams (1 1/2 cup) unthawed frozen strawberries
- 1 banana frozen
- 1/2 tablespoon honey
- 1 1/2 teaspoon lemon juice

Avocado Smoothie:
- 80 ml (1/3 cup) unsweetened almond milk
- 225 grams (1 1/2 cup) chopped avocado
- 2 1/2 tablespoons honey
- 1 tablespoon lemon juice
- 1/3 cup ice cubes
- 1 teaspoon pure vanilla extract

Total Time:
5 mins
Prep Time:
5 mins

Directions

Strawberry Smoothie:

In a blender, combine all the ingredients for the strawberry smoothie and blend until smooth.

Pour evenly into glasses, filling each half way, and place them in the freezer.

Rinse out the blender.

Avocado Smoothie:

Place the remaining ingredients in the blender and blend until smooth.

Assemble:

Use a spoon to gently transfer the avocado smoothie on top of the strawberry smoothie.

Nutrition Information

Amount per serving (250 g) — Calories: 248, Fat: 11.5g, Saturated Fat: 1g, Sodium: 21mg, Carbohydrates: 39.5g, Fiber: 8g, Sugar: 26g, Protein: 1g

31. STRAWBERRY-CARROT SMOOTHIES

Ingredients

- 2 cups (16 ounces) reduced-fat plain Greek yogurt
- 1 cup carrot juice
- 1 cup orange juice
- 1 cup frozen pineapple chunks
- 1 cup frozen unsweetened sliced strawberries

Total Time
Prep/Total Time: 5 min.

Makes

5 servings

Directions
Place all ingredients in a blender; cover and process until smooth.

Nutrition Facts
1 cup: 141 calories, 2g fat (1g saturated fat), 5mg cholesterol, 79mg sodium, 20g carbohydrate (15g sugars, 1g fiber), 10g protein. Diabetic Exchanges: 1 fruit, 1/2 reduced-fat milk.

32. PEACH GREEN TEA SMOOTHIE

Ingredient
- 1 cup chilled green tea
- 1 heaping cup frozen peaches
- 1/2 of a frozen banana
- 1/2 cup plain non-fat Greek yogurt
- 2 tablespoons honey
- 1/2 teaspoon vanilla extract
- 1/2 cup of ice, use less or omit if you want a thinner less frosty smoothie

Total time

5 minutes

Directions

Place all of the ingredients into a blender and blend until smooth.

33. HEALTHY CHOCOLATE BANANA SMOOTHIE

Ingredients
- 1 cup Almond Breeze Chocolate Almond Milk
- 1 tablespoon unsweetened cocoa powder
- 2 frozen banana
- 1 handfull baby spinach about 1/4 cup

Total Time:
5 mins
Prep Time:
5 mins

Direction
In a blender add the chocolate almond milk, unsweetened cocoa powder, frozen banana slices and baby spinach.
Blend until thick and smooth
Serve and enjoy immediately.

Nutrition Facts

Amount Per Serving

Calories 154

% Daily Value*

Total Fat 1.9g 3%

Total Carbohydrate 36.6g 12%

Dietary Fiber 4.4g 18%

Sugars 22.1g

Protein 2.5g 5%

Vitamin A 9%

Vitamin C 25%

34. RASPBERRY ALMOND SMOOTHIE

Ingredients
- 2/3 c. plain Greek yogurt (I like Fage Greek yogurt)
- 2/3 c. almond milk (or any other milk of your preference)
- 2/3 c. frozen raspberries
- 1/4 c. almonds, divided
- 1 Tbsp. honey
- 2 tsp. chia seeds

Total Time
5 min
Prep Time
5 min

Instructions

In a blender add all of the ingredients, reserving a few of the almonds. Blend until smooth and all ingredients are incorporated. Chop the reserved almonds to stir in if desired. Pour and enjoy.

35. CARROT GINGER TURMERIC SMOOTHIE

Ingredients
CARROT JUICE
- 2 cups carrots
- 1 1/2 cups filtered water

SMOOTHIE
- 1 large ripe banana (previously peeled, sliced and frozen // more for a sweeter smoothie)
- 1 cup frozen or fresh pineapple
- 1/2 Tbsp fresh ginger (peeled // 1 small knob yields ~1/2 Tbsp)
- 1/4 tsp ground turmeric (or sub cinnamon)
- 1/2 cup carrot juice
- 1 Tbsp lemon juice (1/2 small lemon yields ~1 Tbsp or 15 ml)
- 1 cup unsweetened almond milk

Total Time
20 minutes
Prep Time
20 minutes

Direction
Make carrot juice by adding carrots and filtered water to a high speed blender and blending on high until completely pureed and smooth. Add more water if it has trouble blending / scrape down sides as needed.

Drape a large, thin dish towel over a mixing bowl and pour over the juice. Then lift up on the corners of the towel and begin twisting and squeezing the juice out until all of the liquid is extracted. Set aside pulp for smoothies, or baked goods (such as carrot muffins).

Transfer carrot juice to a mason jar - will keep for several days, though best when fresh.To the blender add smoothie ingredients and blend on high until creamy and smooth. Add more carrot juice or almond milk if it has trouble blending. Scrape down sides as needed.Taste and adjust flavors as needed, adding more banana or pineapple for sweetness, lemon for acidity, ginger for bite, and turmeric for warmth.

Nutrition information
Calories: 144 Fat: 2.3g Sodium: 112mg Carbohydrates: 32g Fiber: 5g Sugar: 17.5g Protein: 2.4g

36. CUCUMBER-MELON SMOOTHIE

Ingredients
- 2 cups reduced-fat plain Greek yogurt
- 1/3 cup honey
- 3 cups chopped honeydew melon
- 2 medium cucumbers, peeled, seeded and chopped
- 1 to 2 tablespoons fresh mint leaves, optional
- 2 cups crushed ice cubes

Total Time
Prep/Total Time: 15 min.
Makes
6 servings

Directions
Place half of each of the following in a blender: yogurt, honey, melon, cucumber and, if desired, mint. Cover; process until blended. Add 1 cup ice; cover and process until smooth. Pour into three glasses; repeat with remaining ingredients.

Nutrition Facts
1 cup: 155 calories, 2g fat (1g saturated fat), 4mg cholesterol, 48mg sodium, 28g carbohydrate (26g sugars, 2g fiber), 9g protein.

37. THE CREAMIEST BANANA CINNAMON ROLL SMOOTHIE

Ingredients

- 2-3 ice cubes
- 1 frozen banana broken into about 4 pieces
- 3 medjool dates pitted
- 1/4 cup old fashioned oats
- 1/2 tsp ground cinnamon
- 1 tsp chia seeds (optional: see notes)
- 1 tsp pure vanilla essence
- 1 cup milk of choice (I use almond)
- 1/2 cup Greek yogurt or non-dairy yogurt of choice

Total Time
5 mins
Prep Time
5 mins

Directions

Add everything to the blender in the order listed and blend until smooth. Optional add-ins: coffee, protein powder.

Nutrition Facts

Amount Per Serving
Calories 254 Calories from Fat 27
% Daily Value*
Total Fat 3g 5%
Cholesterol 2mg 1%
Potassium 568mg 16%
Total Carbohydrates 51g 17%
Dietary Fiber 6g 24%
Sugars 33g
Protein 8g 16%
Vitamin A 1.8%
Vitamin C 6.2%
Calcium 25.2%
Iron 5.9%

38. VEGAN STRAWBERRY PUDDING

Ingredients

- 3 cups strawberries, stems removed
- 1 cup canned coconut cream
- 1/8 teaspoon salt
- 3 tablespoons maple syrup
- 1/2 teaspoon fresh lime zest
- 1 tablespoon fresh lime juice

Total Time:
5 minutes
Prep Time:
5 minutes

Instructions

Place all ingredients into a blender and puree until creamy and thick. Divide into ramekins or small bowls and place in the fridge; allow to chill for ~1 hour.

Enjoy as is, or top with chopped fresh strawberries.

39. HOMEMADE OAT MILK

Ingredients
- 1 cup rolled oats
- 3 cups water
- 1 – 2 dates
- 1/2 tsp. vanilla extract
- a pinch of salt

Total Time:
5 minutes
Prep Time:
5 minutes

Directions
Add the oats, water, dates, vanilla and salt to a high-speed blender and blend for 15-30 seconds until smooth.

Strain through a nut milk bag or a cheesecloth. The leftover pulp can be used in smoothies to add extra fiber.

Pour into a milk bottle and allow to chill for at least 2 hours before drinking.

40. HEALING CRANBERRY SMOOTHIE

Ingredients

- 1/2 cup water
- 1 cup whole cranberries
- 2 oranges, peeled
- 1 banana, frozen
- 1–2 tablespoons maple syrup

Total Time:
5 minutes
Prep Time:
5 minutes

Directions

Place the ingredients into a high powered blender, like in the order listed: water, cranberries, oranges and banana.

Blend until smooth and creamy. If desired, add in 1-2 tablespoons of maple syrup. Sometimes I want this more tart and sometimes I want things a little sweeter!

Nutrition facts

Serving Size: 1 smoothie
Calories Per Serving: 182
% Daily Value
1% Total Fat 0.5g
Saturated Fat 0.1g
0% Cholesterol 0mg
0% Sodium 4.4mg
16% Total Carbohydrate 46.9g
28% Dietary Fiber 7g
Sugars 29.4g
5% Protein 2.4g

CPSIA information can be obtained
at www.ICGtesting.com
Printed in the USA
BVHW011947300123
657444BV00001B/22